INTERNSHIP & VOLUNTEER OPPORTUNITIES

for People Who Love Music

Kathy Furgang and Adam Furgang

ROSEN PUBLISHING®
New York

Published in 2013 by The Rosen Publishing Group, Inc.
29 East 21st Street, New York, NY 10010

Library of Congress Cataloging-in-Publication Data

Furgang, Kathy.
Internship & volunteer opportunities for people who love music/
Kathy Furgang, Adam Furgang.—1st ed.
      p. cm.—(A foot in the door)
Includes bibliographical references and index.
ISBN 978-1-4488-8296-0 (library binding)
1. Music—Vocational guidance. 2. Internship programs. 3. Voluntarism.
I. Furgang, Adam. II. Title. III. Title: Internship and volunteer opportunities for people who love music.
ML3795. F87 2013
780.23—dc23

2012017976

Manufactured in the United States of America

CPSIA Compliance Information: Batch #W13YA: For further information, contact Rosen Publishing, New York, New York, at 1-800-237-9932.

Contents

High school students like this violinist can help teach music to younger students at camps and in special programs.

Introduction

Most people who love music have deep and lasting memories of it from the time they were young children. Perhaps you have always listened to music since you were a baby. Maybe your parents taught you to sing or play an instrument when you were very young. Or maybe you remember buying your first CD and wishing that you could have been there when it was recorded. Music can provide all of us with enjoyment, lasting memories, and a deep appreciation of the arts and culture. For some people, that is enough. For others, a career in music or in a related industry offers a more lasting way to appreciate music.

Whatever your own personal story about music, it is sure to have shaped your young life. You may be interested in classical, gospel, jazz, country, or rock music. You may be wondering how you can keep that excitement alive in a career.

You may aspire to become a singer in a rock band or a musician in a classical orchestra. You may want to learn how to mix a recording or lay down tracks in a studio. However, you don't necessarily need a lot of technical training in music to pursue a career in this field. You just have to know how to appreciate it. Even people who just love to listen to music can explore a variety of music-related careers.

For ambitious and creative people, there are opportunities to learn about the music world as early as high school. An internship is an experience in which a student or trainee works at a trade to learn about the field. Internships are often unpaid work experiences, and some offer academic credit toward graduation. In addition to internships, there are many opportunities for high school students in volunteer positions. Volunteering at an organization provides valuable experience that may help one land a paying job in music down the road. Both internship and volunteer opportunities can help you get your foot in the door to a rewarding career in the music industry.

There are many ways that high school students can explore music careers through hands-on opportunities. Playhouses and production houses offer opportunities for young people, as do orchestra halls and concert halls. The publishing industry allows young people to explore music journalism, music reviewing, books about music, and the creation of sheet music. The fast-paced field of music production can provide a glimpse into the world of music producers, talent agents, sound engineers, and radio disc jockeys. There are even career opportunities for people who want to bring music to local communities, such as music camp directors, instrument repair and tuning specialists, and music therapists.

Whether you are working at a volunteer job or receiving academic credit for an internship, remember that the experience can help open doors to a fascinating career in the world of music.

Chapter One

WHAT CAN I DO WITH MY LOVE OF MUSIC?

You think about music all the time, and you would love to have the opportunity to work in the field somehow. The jump from wanting to be involved to actually being involved is not as big as you might think. Dive headfirst into the career world, but be aware of what the road might be like at the beginning. The work of a volunteer or intern may not be as glamorous or as easy as you imagine. But don't be discouraged for a minute. If you are willing to put in a little hard work, an internship or volunteer opportunity can be the ticket to your future.

To gain the most from your experience in the music industry, you need to pay attention. Keep your eyes and your ears open to what is going on around you, and you can learn about this fascinating field that influences many people. You may even have contact with talented musicians or get a behind-the-scenes look at how a production is put together.

Your love of music can open doors for you that you never knew existed. Here are some of the benefits of

Teen music lovers can find volunteer or internship opportunities where their talents are needed. Beginning tasks may include setting up a room for rehearsal.

getting your foot in the door as early as high school.

Get to Know the Music Field

A volunteer job or internship does not have to be the job or career path you will stick with forever. But just think about the things you will learn ahead of other students! It may be years before other people end up learning what you will learn in just a few weeks or months. Just by being present inside an organization, you will learn about how people work in the field, what kinds of jobs they do, and why these jobs are important in the field.

If you are working with musicians at a live performance or editing tracks that were previously recorded, there are things to know and procedures to follow. The volunteer or intern is often asked to do labor-intensive jobs such as moving instruments; setting up music stands, chairs, or microphones; or fetching whatever might be needed at the time. If you are working in a business office such as that of a record label, booking agent, promoter, or business manager, you may learn a whole different set of ropes. Getting coffee,

setting up conference room presentations, stuffing enve
mailing promotions, or coming up with ideas for tweets
your tasks. While doing these things, you'll be in the mid
action, learning the structure of the company. Getting to
field at a young age is an experience that will likely
make you a more valuable employee in the future.

Working as an intern or volunteer will give you the
chance to decide what parts of the music field interest you most. Interns and volunteers usually work in
a less pressured environment, so they can evaluate
the field as a whole. For example, you may be able
to socialize with other people about their jobs and
what they like about them. You may learn what makes
the jobs in one department similar to or different from
others in the same company.

While you are on the job, you should definitely focus
on your assigned tasks, but you also have the luxury
of exploring the field as a whole by asking questions
and observing others. Learn what you like and don't
like about the field. You can take your knowledge with
you when it is time to look for a college, technical
school, or your first paying job in the field.

It's Fine to Change Your Mind

Suppose you always dreamed of controlling the
knobs on the engineer board, mixing the sounds
of your favorite band. You would give anything to
be the genius behind their unique sound. So you
get an internship at a recording studio. You learn

a few things about the mixing board. But after observing the extremely long hours the engineers put in, and the amount of painstaking troubleshooting they have to do, you wonder if you truly have the patience required for this job.

Working in a recording studio involves long hours of technical work, but the results can be rewarding. Internships are a great way to find out what you enjoy about the music industry.

You may learn important things about yourself during your internship experience. Most important, you may learn that you have changed your mind about pursuing a particular career. This is not a big deal: it is exactly what the learning experience is all about! You become an intern not only to learn what you might like about the industry, but also what you don't like. Testing out the field can help you decide whether you want to pursue it further when you choose a college or technical school or look for a first job after high school.

If you decide against pursuing a path you thought you wanted, don't think of it as wasted time. It's actually a very good use of time. It's best to figure out that you want to pursue another avenue before you commit a lot of time, money, and effort to a career. Think of this as an experimental time: you are testing a hypothesis about what you *think* you want to do. You are allowed to change your mind as a result of your experiments.

Learn About Educational Programs

Remember that an internship or volunteer job in the music industry is a unique opportunity for a high school student. If you enjoy your internship and are planning to go to college, you can

Student musicians from the Berklee College of Music in Boston, Massachusetts, perform at a youth event at a church.

begin looking at colleges that have good music programs. This will give you a head start on your career. If you think you want to major in music, you can eliminate schools that do not have a music program and focus only on those that do. Or, if you are enthusiastic about your experience in sound engineering and music production, you may look into pursuing technical training at an audio engineering school.

Do I Need a College Degree?

No one can deny that a college degree can give you good opportunities in the working world. But do you absolutely need a college diploma to pursue a career in music? Would it be possible to follow your high school experiences by moving directly into a career? It depends on the career you want to pursue. While a booking agent may achieve success because of his or her connections in the field, rather than his or her college degree, not all professions work this way. Pop singers may not need a college degree, but many classically trained musicians do. Technical careers in music may require their own training and certification. Researching careers in high school is a great way to learn about different fields and what you might need to enter them.

As you intern or volunteer, talk with the other young people. Find out where they went to school and what kinds of classes they took. You may find out about some good programs you had not heard of before. It may be especially helpful to chat with people close to your age because the programs or classes they completed may still be offered.

Build a Great College Application

Imagine you are the person who looks through college applications and decides which candidates have the best qualifications for acceptance to the school. You come across someone who

As you get ready for college, you will find that volunteer work and internships look great on college applications.

would like to be admitted to your music program. She has earned good grades and has already completed an internship at a music studio or volunteered at a local concert hall. You can't think of a reason why you should *not* accept the application.

An internship or volunteer opportunity looks great on a college application. It shows initiative, interest, and the willingness to work hard. Your experience can even work for you beyond just appearing on your application form or résumé. Consider writing about the internship in your application essay. Provide a written recommendation from the supervisor of your volunteer job or internship. Your experience will make your application stand out among a large pile of college applications. You may even get more acceptance letters and have a wider array of colleges to choose from.

However, remember that your grades are an even more important factor than an extracurricular volunteer experience. If you can keep up your grades as well as completing the extracurricular experience, your internship will serve you well.

Chapter Two

HOW TO GET STARTED

Once you have decided that you are ready for an internship or volunteer opportunity in the music world, your search can begin. Whether you are a performer, a behind-the-scenes person, or just a plain old music lover, your search may be a challenge because of your young age. But with perseverance and ingenuity, you can locate an opportunity to gain real-world experience, helping you plant a seed that could grow into an eventual career.

The first thing to do is to enlist the help of a trusted adult, such as a parent or guidance counselor. You may need permission from a parent or teacher to participate in some internships and volunteer opportunities. Therefore, it makes sense to involve an adult in the process from the start.

Think about what it is that you love about music. If you are looking for a job where performers work, consider whether the type of music would matter to you. Do you

This teen musician volunteers at a senior center during a celebration.

need to be around rock performers? Classically trained pianists? Jazz musicians? Brainstorm what your ideal position might be, and don't be afraid to dream.

At the same time, be open to revising your dream because it is possible that you will not get your first choice for your first experience. Might a volunteer job helping a local nursing home book musical entertainment for its elderly residents make you happy? It might not be your first choice, but the experience could benefit you and help you attain your dreams in the future. Booking talent for nightclubs or other entertainment arenas is a serious and competitive field. Why not get some experience wherever you can?

Search High and Low

Once you decide roughly what you are looking for, start an exhaustive search. Be creative. While it doesn't hurt to check classified ads in your local newspaper, you may find that you have to dig a little deeper.

Internships may be listed at the career offices of local schools or libraries. Use these offices' resources. Talk to someone working at a career office and tell him or her what you are looking for. The counselors are usually familiar with the kinds of jobs that are advertised through their office. They may be able to tell you quickly and easily if they know of an internship similar to the one you have in mind. If they do not have what you requested, they may be able to steer you in the right direction and let you know what else is available in terms of music-related internships. Internship listings often describe the skills required of the applicants and the tasks that the intern will be performing. These descriptions can give you a good sense of what an organization is looking for.

Newspapers can also be an excellent source for searching for volunteer opportunities. Instead of just checking the classifieds, however, check local ads, entertainment articles, and events listings. This will give you a good idea of organizations in your area that deal with music. Some areas have free papers or magazines that focus solely on local arts and culture. Pick up a variety of these publications. You might see an ad for a concerts-in-the-park series. Or you could see an ad for a traveling concert, a new music store, or a new production at a local playhouse. Make a list of the related organizations. These are all places that you can call to ask if they accept volunteers or if they know of other places that do. The more you ask around and use every avenue that is open to you, the better your chances of finding a promising opportunity.

Get Chatty About Music

When you are curious about getting involved in a field, it helps to get as much information about it as possible. If you wish to one day become a music teacher, a recording artist, an audio engineer, or a booking agent, seek out people who do those things and try to talk to them. If it is possible, try to set up informational interviews with professionals in person or over the phone. You may find that people are happy and willing to talk about their careers.

An informational interview is a discussion meant to give you information about a job or career field. When

When volunteering or interning in a music studio, young people can learn many new skills from the more experienced people around them.

you conduct an informational interview, you are not hoping to get a job from the person you are interviewing. Instead, you hope to find out what the person's job entails. How much training did he or she need to get the job? Is he or she a trained musician? How important is a college education in this field? These are all possible questions that you might ask a person during an informational interview.

Work with Who You Know

Sometimes the best place to look for a great opportunity is right under your nose. Your own music teacher or local church choir leader may know of interesting opportunities. In addition to asking for ideas from people you know, ask if there is anyone that you might be introduced to who works in the music industry. The people you know may know some fascinating professionals! Even if people don't have these kinds of connections to offer, an informational interview with someone you know can be a worthwhile experience.

Get involved in school and local groups to increase your knowledge and widen your circle of acquaintances. Keeping your options open, asking questions, and asking for help can lead you toward the opportunities you seek.

Make sure to write down your questions before you go to the interview, and then use them to lead the discussion. The person you are interviewing may decide to talk about aspects of the job that you did not ask about. That's all right: you may get valuable information about those parts of the job. Remember that your main purpose is to gain information. If you find that at the end of the interview you still do not have the answers to some basic questions, feel free to circle back and ask them again. However, be mindful of the person's time, and try to keep the discussion under an hour.

When you are done with the interview, you will hopefully feel that you learned about the industry a little bit. This might lead you to want to know more or to try to find other people to talk to. The more questions you ask and the more you learn, the more likely you will be to find an opportunity that suits you.

Expect the Unexpected

When you are looking for internships or volunteer programs in the world of music, remember to be open-minded. Some people start long and interesting careers in areas they never dreamed they would be a part of. The world of music is vast, so think about the many opportunities you might be able to explore. For example, a teen who wants to learn more about the orchestra might instead have an opportunity to be part of a local children's musical production. Sure, there are ukuleles and accordions instead of harps and cellos, but the work is still in the world of music.

Be as open as possible to the opportunities that you read about. Don't think that you can't take a job opportunity because it is not exactly what you want to do with your life. At your age, you

Local stage productions and musicals often use the help of community volunteers to help things run smoothly backstage.

will not be pigeonholed as only being able to work in children's musicals. Instead, the experience from the children's musical may make a statement about your commitment and your hard work. Experiment and have fun! Internships and volunteer opportunities should be fun and rewarding.

Chapter Three

PERFORMING MUSIC

Some music lovers want to get involved in the performing end of the industry. You may have been playing an instrument since you were just learning your alphabet. Being a professional musician may be your life's dream.

Live musical productions are an exciting experience for the performer as well as the audience. The desire to become a professional musician attracts many young people to internships and volunteer jobs in the world of performing arts. Depending on your location, you may be able to become part of some exciting and amazing performances. As a high school student, you could have the honor of observing and assisting talented musicians and performers that you someday hope to emulate.

Playhouses

If you are lucky enough to live in a big city such as New York, Los Angeles, or Chicago, you may have a huge selection of playhouses to explore for internship and volunteer

Students sing, dance, and perform in a production at the Actors' Playhouse in Miami, Florida. Musical productions like these may use volunteers for a variety of tasks.

opportunities. Broadway is one of the most famous places on Earth for the performing arts. You will see professional musicians and singers roaming these streets daily, making a living in the world of music. Just being immersed in such an energetic and creative environment can be a valuable experience for a young musician.

However, while Broadway is great, not everyone lives in a big city, and even those who do may not have the chance to

How to Behave Like an Intern

Volunteers and interns often report to a supervisor who works at the performance venue. This may be a paid employee or a local volunteer in charge of a show. Being on your best behavior on the job is essential, and so is being prompt and responsible. When completing an internship for academic credit, interns may be graded for their work and often have to write papers about their experience. The school usually receives a report about the student's work from the person in charge of the interns.

Even as a volunteer, a good work ethic must be evident to the supervisors. You may think that someone who is not being paid can't get fired, but that's not the case. A volunteer's work is often important and relied upon, so it must be done right. Even though you are an unpaid volunteer, the playhouse or concert hall can always pick from others willing to do your job and do it well.

work on large productions at a young age. That's why small-town playhouses are a great opportunity for a young person to get involved in music. Many playhouses rely on the help of volunteers to put on local productions. They may not have the budget to pay many employees, so some important jobs may be left for volunteers.

Local playhouses may have many different opportunities throughout the year. Remember that live performances are continually changing, so there are many chances to get in and experience one from the start. Productions typically begin with auditions and then go into rehearsals, set design, dress rehearsals, and performances. All this time, musicians are practicing and singers are rehearsing their parts. Check local papers or Web sites for ads for scheduled auditions, and then begin your job search around that time.

A high school student might be involved in a number of tasks, such as set design, costume design, lighting, or managing props. People might be needed to set up chairs and equipment for choruses and instrumentalists. On the days of performances, volunteers might hand out programs or man the refreshment stands. Larger playhouses display artwork for people to look at during intermission and before and after the show. These displays are often coordinated and assembled by volunteers.

Local playhouses put on so many performances that you can be working on one production and have your eye on what you would like to do to help out for the next show. While it is important to focus on the job you were assigned to do and perform it well, it is acceptable to ask a supervisor what other opportunities might be available to volunteers or interns for future productions.

Orchestra and Concert Halls

Concert halls might seem like the most professional place for a musician to be. The beautiful décor, the plush seats, and the chandeliers all add to the distinct feeling of going out for a cultured night of entertainment. While some concert halls are more formal

New York's Carnegie Hall provides an elegant setting for concerts, like this tribute to Motown in 2012. Many small towns also have music venues.

than others, most give you the feeling of being in an exciting place to hear beautiful music. Some of the most talented musicians in the world play in orchestra and concert halls in big cities. Both the large, well-known venues and the ones in small cities and towns can use the help of young people who want to get involved in the world of music.

Holidays are an especially busy time for concert halls because they often have special seasonal performances. Some

Enjoy the Show

While you work in the area of performing arts, keep your love of music alive. Continue to see shows as an audience member as often as you can. Remember that you can learn something by listening to and watching performances by professional musicians. If you hope to become a musician one day, it can be an especially rewarding and fun experience.

If you are working on a show behind the scenes, ask if you can view the performance from the audience just once. Then you will get to see how the show comes together as an art form in the end. You will also get to compare the level of performances of the professional musicians with the orchestra you are used to hearing at school. This can give you an idea of the quality and skill of the work at the professional level.

have stages on which *The Nutcracker* ballet can be performed. These productions take a lot of coordination on the part of community members who publicize and hold auditions, and then support a difficult rehearsal schedule. These are often good places to ask to volunteer and help out. You can learn a lot about the productions in a short period of time.

Performing Arts Centers

Most states have performing arts centers that house larger rock, pop, or country music acts as they tour across the country. A music lover could seek an internship in the offices of one of these

This performance by the Bret Michaels Band is being recorded for a television reality show. Many people are needed to make productions like these happen smoothly.

centers. Employees spend a lot of time scheduling events and organizing opening acts throughout the year. Scheduling of class or group trips and other special events also occurs in the offices of these arenas.

While you may think that an office job is far removed from the creative act of making or performing music, working at a performing arts center can be a good way to learn about certain aspects of the music industry. Ticket sales, performance scheduling, and filling the calendar with dates takes a lot of coordination with bands and their booking agents. In addition, there may be opportunities for young people to get involved in other parts of office life.

Chapter Four

MUSIC PUBLISHING

Did you know that there are hundreds of journals, magazines, newspapers, and other periodicals about music? Think of any instrument, music genre, or music school, and you should be able to find some kind of periodical dedicated to it.

While it is true that publishing centers are often in large cities such as New York, there are publications made in places all over the world. You can find banjo newsletters or bluegrass journals and even a quarterly magazine about the Autoharp. The more you look, the more you will find examples of places where music lovers are working, thinking, and writing about music.

Check out your local library or magazine store to see what they have available. You can also search the Web for interesting music titles. Read the periodicals for pleasure and to learn something about the business. Be sure to check to see where the periodicals are published. There

Issue 1153 >> March 29, 2012
$4.99

Rolling Stone

rollingstone.com

Too Crooked to Fail

THE CRIMES OF BANK OF AMERICA

By Matt Taibbi

The Return of 'Mad Men'

Madonna's Breakup Album

Radiohead's New Groove, New Tour

1945-2012

DAVY JONES

Bruce
The Rolling Stone Interview
By Jon Stewart

Rolling Stone has been one of the most popular music publications since the late 1960s. Many large and small publications around the country may get help from interns or volunteers.

may even be some published near you. Go on a hunt for opportunities and be resourceful.

General Periodicals

Another way to explore music-related publishing is to look for general newspapers or periodicals that include music reviews and discuss music as part of their regular publication. Many local newspapers have an arts section that provides reviews of new CDs, local classical performances, nightclub acts, or popular recording artists who are performing in town that week. These reviews are published in the print or online editions of the periodical. Someone who loves music could pursue a volunteer job or internship at one of these publications. People often specialize in different sections at a newspaper. So specify that you are interested in the entertainment section of the paper, and you will likely get to cover the music business at least some of the time.

The smaller the periodical, the greater the chance that you might be able to write a music review or article about a local event or new CD release. In addition, you may be able to provide background research to staff writers who are working on articles themselves.

Sheet Music

Maybe you remember the first time you learned to read sheet music. You may have been elementary school age or even younger. Maybe you peeked ahead in your music book to see what songs you might learn. Or perhaps you tried to play the new songs in the book before they were assigned to you. If you are truly interested in music, you may have a fond connection with the music books

Many music publishers make sheet music for bands, orchestras, or individual musicians to use when playing their instruments.

and sheet music that students and performers read.

The making of sheet music can be a complicated business. People with a lot of formal musical training are needed to convert songs from the popular versions you hear on radio or television to the ones you use to play your violin, piano, guitar, or even the clarinet.

Music publishers that make sheet music hire talented musicians, but they sometimes also hire interns or volunteers. There are dozens of sheet music publishers in the United States. Leave no stone unturned when you look for opportunities. Even though you will probably not be creating the sheet music or doing the writing, you may be able to work with interesting people who can teach you about the business and what it takes to break into it. Asking questions while you are there will help you learn what education and experience you need to one day do this job.

Books About Music

General publishers create books on countless subjects. If you find a

Learn the Ropes

When you are working at your internship or volunteer position, take in as much as possible. Think about where the assignments originate and who is responsible for getting the work done. The chain of command in an office may be very different from one in a musical production, so learn about the environment you are in. This may help you understand who can teach you the most and whom to approach if you have a question about your work. Try to address the correct person when you have a problem. Learning how the organization is put together can help you do this well.

non fiction book publisher near you, there is a good chance it may publish some books about music. There may even be an editor who concentrates on the company's music books. Many book publishers use interns, and they may be very flexible based on your schedule and academic requirements. In fact, the internship may provide English or other academic credits.

The great thing about internships is that they can be customized to meet your needs. For example, you might have a music teacher contact the publisher to let it know that you need to concentrate on books about music. Your tasks could be as simple as keeping track of photos or illustrations used in the book or helping with paperwork associated with the project. But as with most things, the experience is what you make of it. Be sure to read the manuscript, and notice the changes the editor makes. Try to learn about the subject matter and the process of making a book. Ask questions and get involved. Make an effort to customize your experience to meet your needs. Take advantage of your unique situation and learn as much as you can.

Internships are a great opportunity to learn about more than one thing. While students may seek an internship at a publisher to learn about music, they may find that they learn a great deal about the publishing industry, sparking a whole new interest. Keep your options open when working in an internship. You just might learn something new that could pull you in an exciting new direction.

Chapter Five

IN THE MUSIC BUSINESS

Think of the new music you discover on the radio, the Internet, or at local clubs. It may not be something your parents or teachers love, but you can tell when a new act is great. You know music because you listen to so much of it, and you are excited by new and innovative sounds. There are many opportunities for people like you to get a foot in the door.

Not every music lover is a musician. Plenty of people who love music simply have a great ear for wonderful sounds. Maybe they have a sense of what will become popular or how to spot talent. These people are an important part of the music industry. Executives at record companies can make a lot of money spotting the next big band or recording act. These people had to start somewhere! They, too, were once high school students who were eager to get into the business.

There are so many different jobs to learn about in the music industry that it may be impossible to explore them all. The following are some of the different jobs that people in the industry have. Once you learn what each professional does, you can search for opportunities to work alongside these people on your journey to your own music career.

Booking Agent

A booking agent is also known as a theatrical agent, a booker, or a booking representative. No matter what title is used, this person books venues and schedules performance dates for musical talent. As you can imagine, the draw of the talent will dictate how popular the booking agent is. Booking agents who work with top talent can make millions of dollars annually for booking touring acts in venues around the country and across the world.

A booking agent is very familiar with many arenas and sports venues where bands can play. The agent must be able to estimate how many tickets the artist can sell in each city or town to know how large a venue to book. The idea is to sell as many tickets as possible. At the same time, a sold-out venue looks much better for an artist than one that has half of the seats empty. Therefore, reserving and selling out a slightly smaller venue is better than booking an arena and only filling it halfway.

You can research booking agents by calling local music venues in your area. Make a list of the agents that the venues use. You can then call or write to these agents to ask about volunteer or internship opportunities.

Promoter

A promoter might also be called a talent promoter or a concert promoter. This person or company hosts musical artists at concerts, clubs, and events and coordinates details at the venue. The promoter helps plan and execute the entire concert

Members of the band LMFAO perform in New York City. Promoters and booking agents are involved in scheduling live performances and promoting events to the public.

experience. Questions such as what the stage will look like, how and when the tickets will go on sale, and what kinds of goods will be sold at the event are all issues that the promoter handles.

Another important role of the promoter is to help advertise the artist before, and even during, the performance. The reputation of a band or musical group relies on the work of the promoter. Whether the promoter is working with an unknown band in a small city or a hugely popular band in a giant sports arena in a big city, the work of the promoter is similar. He or she makes the event the best it can be.

Promoters who work with lesser-known performers may be willing to accept high school students for internships or volunteer jobs. Larger promoters may have programs already set up for these purposes.

Sound Technician

Also known as an audio technician or sound operator, the sound technician has to set up and use soundboards and other sound equipment during concerts or live performances. The sound technician's work allows the audience to hear the music and appreciate the show. The soundboards control the different sounds that come from instruments and microphones. Much of the popular music performed today has an electronic aspect to it. The sound technician controls a variety of these electronic sounds by using different channels on the soundboard. If the vocals at a concert are not loud enough and are being drowned out by the guitar or drums, the sound technician is the person who can fix it. Before each show begins, the sound technician

Sound technicians control the levels of different electronic sounds made by musicians in a studio.

tests the sounds that are controlled by the soundboard to make sure they are at the right levels. Sound technicians may use volunteers to help set up or break down equipment while working at a concert or other live performance.

Record Producer

When musicians record their work in a studio, a record producer oversees the production. Producers create albums or individual tracks for artists. They manage and direct the albums, including deciding what tracks will be included and in what order. They oversee the recording sessions and deal with any problems that come up along the way. Even though tracks are now recorded on CD instead of record albums like they were in the past, the term "record producer" has stuck. Producers are still called this name by the general public, as well as by the rest of the music industry.

A record producer's reputation in the recording industry is based on how well the final product comes

One of the music industry's most famous producers, Quincy Jones, poses near a plaque celebrating sales of one of the records he produced—Michael Jackson's blockbuster album *Thriller*.

out. So it is not only the band or artist that can achieve fame from a recording—it's also the producer. A record producer can make a lot of money, depending on the popularity of the artists making the recordings.

If you live near a big city, check with major record labels such as RCA, Sony, Warner Brothers, or Capitol Records for internship opportunities. Otherwise, research smaller, independent record labels for producers who might accept interns or volunteers.

Keep Exploring

In addition to the ones mentioned in this chapter, there are countless other jobs related to the music industry. Seeking out people who work in the field is a helpful way to learn what else you might be interested in. For example, some classically trained musicians may have careers mixing sound at concerts or engineering sounds in a studio. Instead of being the concert pianist you always thought you would be, you might love being a record producer for other concert pianists. The more you look around for opportunities that interest you, the more doors will open. The world of music can have fascinating twists and turns. You just need to be there to be a part of them.

Recording Engineer

Recording engineers are known by many alternate titles. They might be called a mixer, a recording assistant, or an audio engineer. The job of the recording engineer is to manage sound-boards and equipment during studio recording sessions. The engineer carries out the record producer's requests and mixes the sounds to create the best recording possible. Recording engineers are highly trained in their craft and can make music sound shallow, tinny, or rich and can give it different echoes and tones. At times, the work of the recording engineer can make the music sound very different from what the performers were actually playing in the recording studio. Similar to a special effects artist working on a film, the recording engineer can work magic in the studio.

Recording engineers have difficult schedules to maintain and may use interns or volunteers to help them set up recording sessions or manage visitors to the studio. Write letters to recording studios to inquire about engineers who might be looking for extra help.

Disc Jockey

One of the most coveted jobs in the music industry is the disc jockey. The name originated in the days when music was recorded and played on vinyl records called discs. Even though CDs are mainly used to play records today, the name stuck.

A disc jockey, or DJ, works at a radio station playing music according to the station's format. Whether it is gospel, country, rock, or oldies, the DJ usually chooses the selections he or she wants to play and announces them over the airwaves. The job often appears to be glamorous to others because DJs' voices are broadcast over the airwaves and people become familiar with them, like a celebrity. A lot of the training of a disc jockey is on-the-job training. Radio stations can be big or small, depending on their location, the size of their broadcast area, and the size of their audience.

Radio stations may rely on help from community members or interns to help them function and broadcast their music programming. You can also contact local radio stations for information about community events for which disc jockeys might need assistance.

Chapter Six

FOR THE MUSICAL AT HEART

There are many people working in the music world who love music and playing instruments but do not work for a professional orchestra, choir, or concert hall. These people are the ones in your local community whom you probably know best. Music teachers are a great example because they want to pass their love of music on to others. If you explore your community even more, you will find other professionals who help people make music a part of their lives.

Music Camp Jobs

Working at a music camp may be one of the best opportunities for a high school student to get experience in the world of music. A music camp director is the person who runs a music camp's programs for children, usually during the summer months when school is not in session. The camp director establishes the goals for

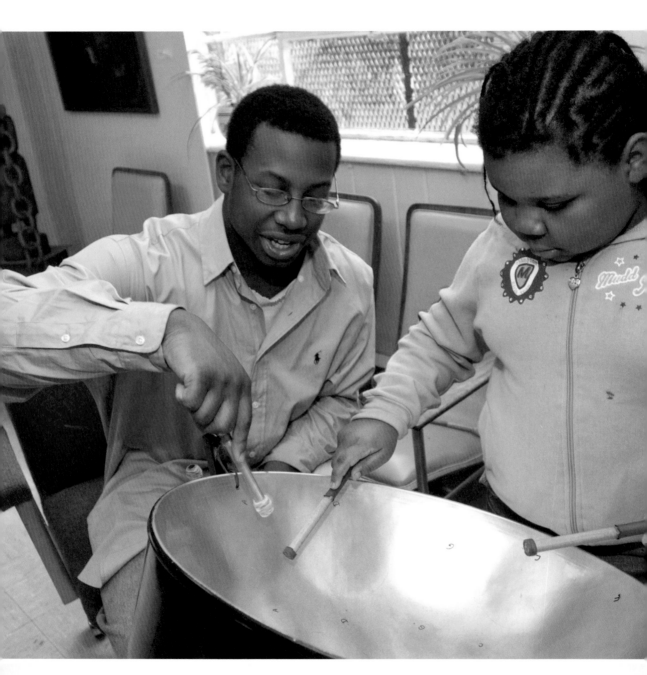

This teen musician volunteers at a neighborhood arts center, where he gives steel drum lessons to younger students.

the program and hires instructors and counselors to work with the children. Your own school or community may offer a music camp during the summer, and you may have even attended these camps in years past.

Teaching young students how to play instruments, sing, or be part of an orchestra or band can be a fun experience. As a counselor, volunteer, or intern, you will most likely work with students who are in elementary school and do not have the skills or experience that you have. Patience is a prerequisite for working with young musicians, but the experience can be very rewarding. It is exciting to see progress on the part of the students from the beginning of the program to the end. Just as you learn to master a song, you can witness young students doing the same thing. At first they may sound as if they will never get the song right, but over time you will slowly work through kinks and help them master every note.

Be aware that summer camp registrations usually start as early as March, so camp directors probably work on their staffing requirements as early as the winter months. Start by speaking with your school's band or orchestra director who can steer you in the right direction. Even if you can not work or volunteer at a program associated with your own school, the camp director may know about other programs that are looking for help.

Making It on Your Own

Many music lovers dream about becoming a famous musician or performer one day. If this is your dream, too, know that an internship can help you meet any goal you have in mind. Whether you become famous one day or not, the work you do in an internship or volunteer opportunity is bound to teach you skills you can use later on in your career. So use your experience to enrich your own dreams. If you research some of the famous musicians you admire, you may find that they had a long journey to becoming recognized in the field. Remember that no one starts out at the top, and everyone can benefit from the kinds of experiences you are seeking.

Once you find a program you are interested in, approach the camp director by phone or e-mail. Ask to set up an appointment to talk about the program and possible work or volunteer opportunities. You may need a written recommendation from your school or from an outside music teacher. There may even be auditions to make sure that the staff working with the children are skilled enough to be able to teach what they know to younger students.

The chance to work at a music camp can be a valuable experience for a young person who wants to learn skills in leadership, teaching, and music. It's also a fun way to spend your summer!

Instrument Repair and Tuning

If you play a musical instrument, you've probably been to a shop where musical instruments are repaired or tuned. These shops may also sell and rent instruments to customers and local schools. You may not have thought of it, but a store like this can be a great place to get a musical volunteer experience. For example, a store may be looking for extra help if it offers

Student interns and volunteers can learn from people who do skilled instrument repair or tuning. These people often work in local music stores or for instrument dealers.

workshops or events for the public. The store may even need extra help around the holidays.

Working at this kind of business allows you to be surrounded by music and musical instruments all day. This is a great opportunity for someone who loves the technical end of music and wants to learn how musical instruments are put together to create sound. While you may know how to tune your own piano, guitar, or other instrument, a professional tuner must know as much as possible about all kinds of instruments. Learning from these professionals is a valuable experience for a young person.

Music Therapy

One of the least recognized fields in the music world is music therapy. This job is considered one of the health professions, but it is a wonderful job for a music lover who enjoys helping people.

A music therapist might work in a private practice or even in a hospital. The therapist's job is to treat patients with emotional, social, physical, and cognitive problems by using music. The therapy may include moving to music, listening to music to help the patient's mood, or even singing with the patient. Studies have found that humans react in a unique way when they hear music. Music often conjures up special emotions that can be used to help heal suffering patients. Music therapy is often used to treat symptoms of depression or anger issues, helping support people through difficult times. It can also be used to help patients recover their movement and language abilities after a stroke or brain injury. A music therapist is a caring and patient person who stays current with new therapies or experiences that can help his or her patients.

A music therapist at Dana-Farber Cancer Institute plays the guitar and sings for a four-year-old patient, who plays along on the bongo drums.

A young person in high school might find a way to work with a music therapist as an internship experience. With an internship experience like this, the student may help create his or her own curriculum. For example, you might work with a guidance counselor or music teacher to write down what you hope to learn about the profession and music's effects on patients. Some of the job might include doing formal research and writing papers about the field. You might then use examples of specific patients you observed and how you think these patients are responding to the treatments.

Getting Academic Credit

One of the big differences between internships and volunteer jobs is that internships are often done for academic credit and sometimes even a grade for your work. Your internship may require meeting periodically with a school adviser to give him or her an update on your work, progress, and learning experiences. Very often, internships involve writing papers to describe your experiences and to reflect upon what you learned. This is a great chance for you to think about what the experience has meant to you and to decide whether it has met your expectations.

If your adviser is a music teacher or guidance counselor, that person may give you additional help in making sense of your experience. The person who is guiding your internship can also be a valuable source of information about where you might want to head in the future. Take advantage of your adviser, and ask as many questions as you can. Your adviser may be able to help you research additional experiences that will foster your knowledge and love of music.

Chapter Seven

MAKE THE MOST OF YOUR INTERNSHIP OR VOLUNTEER OPPORTUNITY

The music industry offers countless jobs and fascinating opportunities in which a young person can grow. When looking for an internship or volunteer position, first think about your location. Remember that large cities will have the biggest concert halls, performance theaters, and recording studios. These venues are more likely to have established internship programs. However, also remember that venues in a smaller town may offer just as many, or even more, opportunities for hands-on involvement in projects. Choose what you feel is best for you and then go after the job with enthusiasm.

An internship opportunity can have great influence on a young person. It may influence where you go to school and what you decide to major in. If you enjoy your internship or volunteer job, you may decide to look for colleges with strong programs in music or music-related industries. You may wish to focus on a particular aspect of music

At this audition, people sing and act for the director. Auditions are held for productions in small community theaters as well as in large venues and playhouses.

as a specialty. While interning, ask the people you meet where they went to college or technical school and what they majored in. You'll probably find that there are many good programs out there. However, you may also learn that no college major really prepares you for the job you want to do. Many people foster their own careers through apprenticeships or on-the-job training. Getting involved, asking these kinds of questions, and learning new things can help you get a solid start in the music career of your choice.

Be a Good Sport

As a volunteer or intern, you may be asked to do some of the most boring or menial tasks in the office or concert hall. Don't let this worry or discourage you. You can't expect to choose head-line acts or audition the next superstar while you are a volunteer or intern. Often, the work of an intern can be unglamorous and thankless. But make the most of your tasks. If you are setting up seating for an audition, try to take a peek at some of the talent and listen to what they are playing or singing. Find out which companies are used to provide instruments or do tuning or repair work for the orchestra. Just learn as much as you can about the process. Be alert, ask questions, and be curious about what you are doing. Your observations can help you decide what you think about the business overall.

While you are being a good sport about the tasks of your volunteer job or internship, think about the future. You may want to ask about other internship opportunities that are available for people your age. If people get to know you and realize that you are a hardworking, responsible person, they may be willing to give you another learning opportunity in the future. The

Mentors who can provide on-the-job training may also be able to give letters of recommendation for colleges and job interviews.

next time around, you may be given more responsibility or a job that uses the skills you have already learned.

Look for Recommendations

An internship or volunteer job is valuable in so many ways. In addition to the experience you are gaining, you are also meeting people who can write you those all-important recommendation letters that you will need as you apply to college or other jobs. A supervisor or other adult who can write a recommendation letter is a valuable asset to you at the beginning of your career. Someone who has witnessed your work firsthand is uniquely able to write about your personal qualities and work habits. The position of the person writing the letter also carries some weight and distinction. Think about how impressive a recommendation letter from a record executive could look on your college application. Think about how that letter might help you get a paying job at another studio.

The people you meet along your career path can be valuable resources. That's why it is so important to make a good impression when you take on an internship or volunteer job. If the supervisor or other employees see you as a hard worker and a good and friendly person, you are building a good reputation in the business. People move from company to company, and it is possible that the people you are working with at one organization know the employees at another. Your name may be mentioned if you are looking for work in the future. People may recognize your name when they hear it. You want their memories of you to be positive ones so that they can say, "I know that person. He was a great intern at my last job. He's reliable and smart, and he's a quick learner." A personal, unofficial recommendation like that could be just what you need to land a job. So act as professionally as you can at all times.

Put a Résumé Together

If you wrote down everything you have ever done that was related to music, how long would your list be? Some people can make huge lists of every concert, play, or performance they have appeared in. Try creating a résumé of experiences you have had in music. Be sure to include any achievements you are especially proud of. Your résumé can help a college admissions

A résumé that includes internship and volunteer work in the area you wish to pursue can make your experience stand out to a potential employer.

officer or employer see your level of knowledge about or talent in music. Include any internship or volunteer programs you have participated in, and include a brief description of your responsibilities and accomplishments on the job.

Show the résumé to a guidance counselor so that you can get help formatting the document correctly and wording your experiences in the best possible way. A guidance counselor has seen many résumés and can help you make yours more appealing to a school or employer. Some guidance offices even have books about how to organize a résumé correctly. A well-constructed résumé is a valuable tool for showing people the range and quality of your experiences.

Connect with a Mentor

Finding people who share your interests can be challenging but rewarding. A mentor is an experienced person who can guide you and take you under his or her wing as you are learning something new. A mentor can help you launch your career by helping you find appropriate training and job opportunities. An adult who is already in the business can be a great mentor and provide feedback and advice for the future.

Feel Good About It All

Internships and volunteer opportunities in your local community are a great way to jump-start any career. But you can always begin learning about the music industry, whether you get your dream internship or not. You can feel good that you are taking action that will eventually lead you in the right direction. Read books and magazines about the industry and the jobs you are interested in. Read about colleges and special programs that teach the skills you want to learn. Remember that you have a head start just by taking these steps to become familiar with the field.

Glossary

academic credit Recognition by a college or school that a student has fulfilled a requirement leading to a diploma.

applicant One who applies for something, such as a career position or entry into a school.

booking agent A person who secures performance engagements for musical artists.

classified ad A short advertisement in a newspaper or magazine that appears under headings with others of the same type, such as job openings or items for sale.

disc jockey A person at a radio station who introduces and plays music recordings, news reports, commercials, and other programming on the air.

guidance counselor A school professional who advises students on academics, careers, and post–high school educational options.

informational interview An interview with a professional designed to gather information and details about a profession or other topic.

intern A student or trainee who works in a particular occupation, usually without pay and sometimes for school credit.

music camp director A person who runs a camp dedicated to teaching and learning music.

music producer A person who works with recording artists and record labels to make recordings or albums.

music therapist A health professional who uses music as treatment for illnesses, disabilities, or other health issues.

periodical A magazine, journal, or newspaper that is published on a regular basis.

promoter A person who organizes, advertises, presents, and often finances concerts at performance venues.

recommendation letter A letter written about someone to recommend his or her work or personal qualities to a prospective employer or school.

recording engineer A person who manages soundboards and equipment during studio recording sessions.

résumé A document that lists a person's education, qualifications, and previous work experiences.

sound technician A person who is responsible for high-quality sound during a concert or live performance, including setting up and using sound equipment.

volunteer To work for an organization without pay.

For More Information

Afro American Music Institute (AAMI)
7131 Hamilton Avenue
Pittsburgh, PA 15208
(412) 241-6775
Web site: http://afroamericanmusic.org
This organization offers many educational programs for youth interested in learning about music from an African American
perspective.

American Music Therapy Association (AMTA)
8455 Colesville Road, Suite 1000
Silver Spring, MD 20910
(301) 589-3300
Web site: http://www.musictherapy.org
The AMTA helps guide the development of the therapeutic use of
music in rehabilitation, special education, and community set-
tings. The organization is committed to the advancement of
education, training, professional standards, credentials, and
research in the music therapy field.

Billboard Magazine
770 Broadway
New York, NY 10003
Web site: http://www.billboard.com
Billboard Magazine and its online home, Billboard.com, are a pri-
mary source of information on trends and innovation in music,

serving music fans, artists, executives, tour promoters, publishers, radio programmers, lawyers, retailers, digital entrepreneurs, and many others. Internships are available to students in a variety of departments.

Canadian Academy of Recording Arts and Sciences (CARAS)
345 Adelaide Street West, 2nd Floor
Toronto, ON M5V 1R5
Canada
(416) 485-3135
Web site: http://www.carasonline.ca
This organization's goal is to showcase and promote Canadian music and the achievements of Canadian artists.

GRAMMY Foundation
3030 Olympic Boulevard
Santa Monica, CA 90404
(310) 392-3777
Web site: http://www.grammyfoundation.org
The GRAMMY Foundation cultivates the appreciation of the role of recorded music in American culture. It offers a music industry camp in three cities for selected high school students. The ten-day summer program culminates in media projects, CD recordings, and showcase performances.

Hear the Music Live
12672 Limonite Avenue, Suite 3E-303
Eastvale, CA 92880

(800) 657-1320

Web site: http://www.hearthemusiclive.org

This nonprofit organization works with foster care homes to send teens and preteens to local concerts and give them opportunities to meet artists.

League of American Orchestras

33 West 60th Street, 5th Floor

New York, NY 10023

(212) 262-5161

Web site: http://www.americanorchestras.org

The League of American Orchestras leads, supports, and champions America's orchestras and the vitality of the music they perform. The league links a national network of instrumentalists, conductors, managers and administrators, board members, business partners, and volunteers.

National Association for Music Education (NAfME)

1806 Robert Fulton Drive

Reston, VA 20191

(800) 336-3768

Web site: http://www.nafme.org

NAfME's mission is to advance music education by encouraging the study and making of music by all. The organization supports music teachers and helps promote and guide music study as an integral part of the school curriculum.

Its Web site provides resources for people interested in music careers.

National Association of Music Merchants (NAMM)
5790 Armada Drive
Carlsbad, CA 92008
(760) 438-8001
Web site: http://www.namm.org
NAMM's mission is to strengthen the music products industry and promote the pleasures and benefits of making music. Members are musical instrument stores and their suppliers. The organization's trade shows serve as a hub for people wanting to seek out the newest innovations in musical products, recording technology, sound, and lighting.

National Organization of Record Industry Professionals (NARIP)
P.O Box 2446
Toluca Lake, CA 91610-2446
(818) 769-7007
Web site: http://www.narip.com
The NARIP promotes education, career advancement, and goodwill among record industry professionals.

Playing for Change Foundation
P.O. Box 1505
Culver City, CA 90232

Web site: http://playingforchange.org

The Playing for Change Foundation is dedicated to connecting the world through music by providing resources to musicians and their communities around the world. The foundation strives to create positive social change through music education. Volunteers can help organize nonprofit music benefit concerts and other fundraisers.

San Francisco Opera
301 Van Ness Avenue
San Francisco, CA 94102
(415) 864-3330
Web site: http://sfopera.com

The San Francisco Opera is the second-largest opera company in North America. It provides a wide variety of opportunities for interns and volunteers to experience the magic of opera; meet new people; and gain practical, hands-on experience in artistic and administrative areas.

SunFest
525 Clematis Street
West Palm Beach, FL 33401
(561) 659-5980
Web site: http://sunfest.com

SunFest is Florida's largest waterfront music and art festival, featuring well-known pop, rock, and jazz acts, as well as up-and-comers. The annual festival uses many student volunteers, who can earn community service credit for their work.

Volunteer Canada
353 Dalhousie Street, 3rd Floor
Ottawa, ON K1N 7G1
Canada
(613) 231-4371
Web site: http://volunteer.ca
Volunteer Canada works to strengthen the involvement of citizens, including youth, in volunteer service.

Web Sites

Due to the changing nature of Internet links, Rosen Publishing has developed an online list of Web sites related to the subject of this book. This site is updated regularly. Please use this link to access the list:

http://www.rosenlinks.com/FID/Music

For Further Reading

Allen, Paul. *Artist Management for the Music Business.* 2nd ed. Boston, MA: Focal Press, 2011.

Chertkow, Randy, and Jason Feehan. *The Indie Band Survival Guide: The Complete Manual for the Do-It-Yourself Musician.* New York, NY: St. Martin's Griffin, 2008.

Field, Shelly. *Career Coach: Managing Your Career in the Music Industry* (Ferguson Career Coach). New York, NY: Ferguson, 2008.

Gordon, Steve R. *The Future of the Music Business: How to Succeed with the New Digital Technologies: A Guide for Artists and Entrepreneurs* (MusicPro Guides). 3rd ed. Milwaukee, WI: Hal Leonard Books, 2011.

Harmon, Daniel E. *How to Start Your Own Band* (Garage Bands). New York, NY: Rosen Central, 2012.

Hasan, Heather. *How to Produce, Release, and Market Your Music* (Garage Bands). New York, NY: Rosen Central, 2012.

Hatschek, Keith. *How to Get a Job in the Music Industry.* Boston, MA: Berklee Press, 2007.

King, Mike, and Jonathan Feist. *Music Marketing: Press, Promotion, Distribution, and Retail.* Boston, MA: Berklee Press, 2009.

Krasilovsky, M. William, Sidney Shemel, John M. Gross, and Jonathan Feinstein. *This Business of Music: The Definitive Guide to the Music Industry.* 10th ed. New York, NY: Billboard Books, 2007.

Passman, Donald S. *All You Need to Know About the Music Business.* 7th ed. New York, NY: Free Press, 2009.

Rutter, Paul. *The Music Industry Handbook* (Media Practice).
New York, NY: Routledge, 2011.

Thall, Peter M. *What They'll Never Tell You About the Music Business: The Myths, the Secrets, the Lies (& a Few Truths)*.
New York, NY: Billboard Books, 2010.

Wixen, Randall D. *The Plain and Simple Guide to Music Publishing*. 2nd ed. Milwaukee, WI: Hal Leonard, 2009.

Wooster, Patricia. *Music Producer* (21st Century Skills Library).
Ann Arbor, MI: Cherry Lake Publishing, 2012.

Bibliography

Aksomitis, Linda. *Choosing a Career* (Issues That Concern You). Farmington Hills, MI: Greenhaven Press, 2009.

Bolles, Richard Nelson, Carol Christen, and Jean M. Blomquist. *What Color Is Your Parachute? For Teens: Discovering Yourself, Defining Your Future.* Berkeley, CA: Ten Speed Press, 2006.

CareersinMusic.com. "Recording & Record Industry Jobs." Retrieved March 3, 2012 (www.careersinmusic.com/music -jobs.aspx).

Coon, Nora. *Teen Dream Jobs: How to Get the Job You Really Want Now!* Hillsboro, OR: Beyond Words Publishing, 2003.

Crouch, Tanja. *100 Careers in the Music Business.* 2nd ed. Hauppauge, NY: Barron's Educational Series, 2008.

Eberts, Marjorie, and Margaret Gisler. *Careers for Culture Lovers & Other Artsy Types* (VGM Careers for You). 2nd ed. Lincolnwood, IL: VGM Career Horizons, 1999.

Farr, J. Michael, and Laurence Shatkin. *250 Best Jobs Through Apprenticeships.* Indianapolis, IN: JIST Works, 2005.

Ferguson Publishing. *Careers in Focus: Arts & Entertainment.* 2nd ed. New York, NY: Ferguson, 1999.

Field, Shelly. *Career Opportunities in the Music Industry.* 6th ed. New York, NY: Ferguson, 2010.

Goldberg, Jan. *Careers for Geniuses & Other Gifted Types* (VGM Careers for You series). Chicago, IL: VGM Career Books, 2001.

McDonald, Heather. "What's the Difference Between Mixing and Mastering?" About.com, 2012. Retrieved March 7, 2012 (http://musicians.about.com/od/musiciansfaq/f/mixingor master.htm).

National Association for Music Education. "Career Center: Career Glossary." 2012. Retrieved March 7, 2012 (http://www.menc.org/careers/view/career-center-career-glossary).

Wyckoff, Claire. *Top Careers in Two Years: Communications and the Arts.* New York, NY: Ferguson, 2007.

Index

A

academic credit, 6, 27, 56

B

booking agents, 9, 14, 19, 20, 41
books about music, publishers of,
    6, 37–39
Broadway, 26
business managers, 9

C

Capitol Records, 46
career choices, changing your
    mind about, 10–12
children's productions/musicals,
    23–24
choir leaders, 22
college applications, 15–16, 61,
    62–64
college music programs, 12–15, 59
concert halls, 6, 28–30, 57

D

disk jockeys, 6, 47–48

G

guidance counselors, 17, 19, 56, 64

H

holidays, 29–30, 54

I

independent record labels, 46
informational interviews, 20–23
instrument repair, 6, 53–54
instrument tuning, 6, 53–54
internships and volunteer
    opportunities
    academic credit, 6, 27, 56
    benefits, 9–16
    explanation, 6
    how to behave, 27
    how to find, 17–24
    and parental permission, 17
    type of work/responsibilities,
        7, 9, 28, 59

M

mentors, 64
music camp directors, 6, 49–52
music camps, 6, 49–52
music industry
    education and training
        needed, 14
    getting to know, 9–10
music teachers, 20, 22, 38,
    49, 56
music therapy, 6, 54–56

About the Authors

Kathy and Adam Furgang have collaborated on several books for Rosen Publishing. Adam has been making experimental electronic music for over ten years. He uses synthesizers, computers, and, more recently, iPhones and iPads to create his work. Kathy grew up playing the flute and is now an author who has written dozens of books for the educational market. The Furgangs live in upstate New York with their two sons.

Photo Credits